SKILLED TRADE CAREERS
MECHANICS

by Gary Sprott

Rourke
Educational Media

A Division of
Carson
Dellosa
Education®

Before Reading: *Building Background Knowledge and Vocabulary*

Building background knowledge can help children process new information and build upon what they already know. Before reading a book, it is important to tap into what children already know about the topic. This will help them develop their vocabulary and increase their reading comprehension.

Questions and Activities to Build Background Knowledge:

1. Look at the front cover of the book and read the title. What do you think this book will be about?
2. What do you already know about this topic?
3. Take a book walk and skim the pages. Look at the table of contents, photographs, captions, and bold words. Did these text features give you any information or predictions about what you will read in this book?

Vocabulary: *Vocabulary Is Key to Reading Comprehension*

Use the following directions to prompt a conversation about each word.

- Read the vocabulary words.
- What comes to mind when you see each word?
- What do you think each word means?

Vocabulary Words:
- *automotive*
- *diagnose*
- *hybrid*
- *pneumatic*
- *transmission*
- *vocational*

During Reading: *Reading for Meaning and Understanding*

To achieve deep comprehension of a book, children are encouraged to use close reading strategies. During reading, it is important to have children stop and make connections. These connections result in deeper analysis and understanding of a book.

 Close Reading a Text

During reading, have children stop and talk about the following:

- Any confusing parts
- Any unknown words
- Text to text, text to self, text to world connections
- The main idea in each chapter or heading

Encourage children to use context clues to determine the meaning of any unknown words. These strategies will help children learn to analyze the text more thoroughly as they read.

When you are finished reading this book, turn to the next-to-last page for
After Reading Questions and an **Activity**.

TABLE OF CONTENTS

On the Job...4

What's in My Toolbox?..........................16

Learning the Trade...............................22

Memory Game...30

Index..31

After Reading Questions.....................31

Activity 31

About the Author 32

ON THE JOB

Is your curiosity revved up by machines and things that move, such as cars and motorcycles? Do you like to take things apart to see how they work? How about using super-smart computers to find and fix problems?

If you are thinking, "Yes, yes, and yes!" then you probably want to learn more about mechanics.

Who's Under the Hood?

Did you know there are 1.3 billion cars and trucks in the world? Lots of cars means lots of mechanics—770,000 just in the United States.

Mechanics discuss problems and solutions with car owners before making repairs.

Mechanics are skilled workers who make sure engines, gears, brakes, and other mechanical systems perform properly. They **diagnose** problems by looking, listening, and asking questions. They do tests and follow checklists to keep machinery humming along safely.

diagnose (dye-uhg-NOHS): to determine what the cause of a problem is

You're probably familiar with **automotive** mechanics. Maybe you've seen them change the oil on your family's car or fix a flat tire on the side of the road. But there are many types of mechanics. Some repair trains, boats, or massive construction equipment; others keep aircraft running smoothly.

automotive (aw-tuh-MOH-tiv): relating to or concerning motor vehicles, such as cars

Ready for Battle!

Military mechanics keep armies rumbling along. These specialists inspect and repair armored vehicles that carry troops, equipment, and supplies. They make sure cannons and other large weapons are ready to fire.

Mechanics get special training to work on different types of vehicles or machinery.

At Henry Ford's factory, a new Model T could be built in less than six hours!

Automobiles began replacing horse-drawn carriages more than 100 years ago. And automobiles have been breaking down ever since!

In the early 1900s, the famous Ford Model T was cheap enough (as little as 290 dollars!) to allow lots of people to own cars. More cars led to more repairs. That led to more jobs for mechanics.

In the 21st century, many cars are like computers on wheels. Mechanics need to understand the complex electronic systems that control what a vehicle does and when. They may work on battery-powered electric cars or **hybrid** vehicles that do less damage to the environment.

hybrid (HYE-brid): a type of car powered by more than one means, such as by gasoline and by electricity

Electric vehicles can be plugged in and charged—just like a smartphone!

There are not a lot of women mechanics. But that number has been growing in recent years. Organizations such as Women in Auto Care provide scholarships and education to encourage girls to join the industry.

Change the Oil, Your Majesty!

During World War II, women did many skilled trade jobs while men served in combat. Even the future Queen Elizabeth II of the United Kingdom trained as a mechanic!

WHAT'S IN MY TOOLBOX?

From little lawnmowers to giant jets, mechanics work on machines that are marvels of moving parts. Keeping those engines running can be tricky. A mechanic needs special tools for every situation.

Next Floor, Auto Repair!

Ever tried to lift a car? Don't—it's heavier than a hippopotamus! Mechanics use special lifts to raise cars off the floor to make repairs. (Oh, and don't ever try to lift a hippo either!)

Car lifts give mechanics lots of elbow room and help keep them safe.

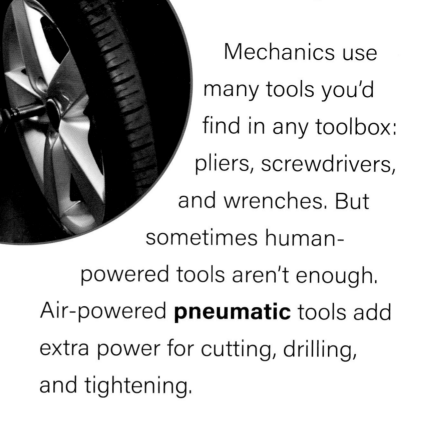

Mechanics use many tools you'd find in any toolbox: pliers, screwdrivers, and wrenches. But sometimes human-powered tools aren't enough. Air-powered **pneumatic** tools add extra power for cutting, drilling, and tightening.

pneumatic (noo-MAT-ik): powered and operated by compressed air

Is your family's car making clunking noises? It could be the **transmission**. High-tech cars and machinery hold clues about why things go wrong. Mechanics use computer diagnostic systems to read electronic codes and pinpoint the cause of the trouble.

transmission (tranz-MISH-uhn): the system in vehicles that shifts gears to make sure different amounts of power get to the wheels to drive at different speeds

Computers help mechanics
find problems under the hood.

LEARNING THE TRADE

So, you're interested in becoming a mechanic? Terrific! Where should you start? In the classroom, of course!

Mechanics must study many subjects and master many skills. Math? Check. Computers and electronics? Double check.

Learning about robotics can help students understand how self-driving cars work.

Some high schools offer classes in auto repair and other types of mechanics. After high school, your next stop may be a **vocational** or technical college. At these schools, students split their time between studying in class and working in a repair shop.

vocational (voh-KAY-shuh-nuhl): relating to a job, profession, or occupation

Future mechanics learn on the job by observing experienced mechanics. They build know-how by starting with simpler tasks. Eventually, they can perform inspections and repairs without supervision.

Hands-on practice can begin early under an expert mechanic's watchful eye.

Master technicians are experts in many areas of automobile mechanics.

Learning doesn't stop for mechanics after they get a job. Technology and standards are always changing. The National Institute for Automotive Service Excellence offers more than 40 tests for different tasks. When they pass the tests, mechanics get an ASE certificate and can earn more money.

Mechanics United

The International Association of Machinists and Aerospace Workers (IAM) includes many automotive professionals. It is one of the largest labor unions in North America.

MEMORY GAME

Look at the pictures. What do you remember reading on the pages where each image appeared?

INDEX

automobiles 11
college 25
computer(s) 4, 12, 20, 21, 22
engines 7, 16

machinery 7, 9, 20
oil 8, 15
repair(s) 6, 8, 11, 16, 25, 26
tools 16, 19

AFTER READING QUESTIONS

1. How many mechanics are there in the U.S.?

2. What are some ways mechanics diagnose problems?

3. What do military mechanics do?

4. Why is it important for mechanics to keep learning?

5. What famous person trained as a mechanic during World War II?

ACTIVITY

Does your family own a car, truck, or van? Ask an adult to let you take a peek under the hood—staying safe at all times, of course! Where is the engine? How about the transmission, radiator, and battery? Spend some time reading the owner's manual for the vehicle. Write down five fascinating things you learned.

ABOUT THE AUTHOR

Gary Sprott is a writer in Tampa, Florida. He has written books about ancient cultures, plants, animals, and automobiles. Gary knows how to jumpstart his minivan or change a tire. But for any other repairs, he knows a really good mechanic!

www.rourkeeducationalmedia.com

PHOTO CREDITS: page 1: ©jirkaejc / iStockphoto.com; page 1: ©xresch / Pixabay; page 3: ©fcafotodigital / iStockphoto.com; page 4: ©Kurhan / iStockphoto.com; page 5: ©dragana991 / iStockphoto.com; page 6: ©viafilms / iStockphoto.com; page 8: ©shorrocks / iStockphoto.com; page 9: ©mikvivi / iStockphoto.com; page 10: ©shaunl / iStockphoto.com; page 12: ©Tramino / iStockphoto.com; page 13: ©Sjoerd van der Wal / iStockphoto.com; page 14: ©Popperfoto / gettyimages.com; page 15: ©Robert Byron / iStockphoto.com; page 17: ©Minerva Studio / iStockphoto.com; page 18: ©kupicoo / iStockphoto.com; page 19: ©sykono / iStockphoto.com; page 21: ©Nikola Ilic / iStockphoto.com; page 23: ©monkeybusinessimages / iStockphoto.com; page 24: ©JohnnyGreig / iStockphoto.com; page 28: ©LindaJohnsonbaugh / iStockphoto.com

Edited by: Madison Capitano
Cover design by: Rhea Magaro-Wallace
Interior design by: Book Buddy Media

Library of Congress PCN Data

Mechanics / Gary Sprott
(Skilled Trade Careers)
ISBN 978-1-73163-833-5 (hard cover)
ISBN 978-1-73163-910-3- (soft cover)
ISBN 978-1-73163-987-5 (e-Book)
ISBN 978-1-73164-064-2 (e-Pub)
Library of Congress Control Number: 2020930170

Rourke Educational Media
Printed in the United States of America
01-1942011937